CONTENTS

Any words appearing in the text in bold, **like this**, are explained in the glossary. You can also look out for them in the Word Bank box at the bottom of each page.

A BUSINESSMAN'S SECRET

Greville Wynne was a man with a secret. He was not just a British businessman – he also worked for British **intelligence**. As a businessman, Wynne sometimes travelled to foreign countries. In 1960, he visited the **Soviet Union**. There he met a **Soviet** army colonel called Oleg Penkovsky. The colonel wanted to spy for the **West** and he gave Wynne a letter to give to British intelligence. The two men soon began working together. They told British and US intelligence secrets about the Soviet **military**.

A dangerous game

Wynne and Penkovsky knew spying was dangerous. They could be sent to prison or executed if Soviet officials caught them. One day, in November 1962, Wynne was in Budapest, Hungary. Four Soviet **agents** approached him on the street. One of the men tripped Wynne up. The agents then threw him into a car. Wynne tried to call for help, but the men hit him on the head and knocked him out.

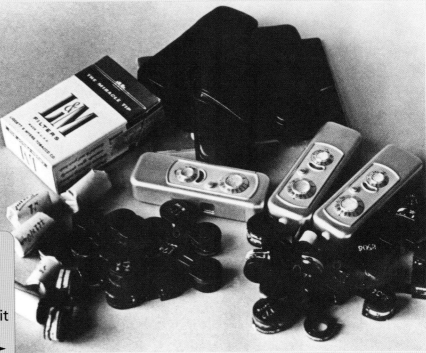

The Soviet Union said that Oleg Penkovsky used spy cameras and rolls of film that were small enough to fit inside a cigarette packet. →

Word Bank **Communism** political system controlled by one party that severely limits personal freedom. Communists believe in this system.

Jailed

Wynne was taken to the Soviet Union and charged with **espionage**. After being questioned, he told his captors that he knew Penkovsky, but not that he was a spy. Wynne was **tried** and sentenced to eight years in prison, but after only two years he was swapped for a Russian spy known as Gordon Lonsdale, who was being held by the American **CIA**. Wynne was lucky. Penkovsky was caught by Soviet agents and executed in 1963 for spying against his country.

After serving two years in prison for spying, Greville Wynne (centre, in overcoat) was released in 1964.

Find out later

Who first used the phrase "Iron Curtain"?

Why were these supplies being **airlifted** into a German city in 1948?

Which two world leaders helped to end the Cold War?

intelligence government services that spy on other countries; also, the information spies gather

THE COLD WAR BEGINS

The Cold War conflict had deep roots. In November 1917, Russians who supported **Communism** had taken control of their country. They later renamed Russia the **Soviet Union**, also known as the USSR. The **Soviet** leaders hoped to spread Communism around the world. However, most Western nations were against Communism. They believed **democracy** and **capitalism** were better.

Spying on "friends"

In September 1939, Germany started World War II by invading Poland. By 1942, many Western nations and the Soviet Union were fighting together against Germany. But there was little trust between Western countries and the Soviet Union. They had been spying on each other before World War II began and the spying did not stop during the war, even though they were now supposed to be on the same side.

British Prime Minister Winston Churchill (front left) meets with US President Franklin Roosevelt (front centre) and Soviet leader Joseph Stalin (front right), several months before the end of World War II.

Word Bank   capitalism   economic system that allows people to own property and business
democracy   political system that allows people to elect their leaders

The Iron Curtain

In May 1945, World War II ended in Europe. By the time the fighting stopped, the Soviet army was in control of most of eastern Europe. The Western nations wanted to limit Soviet power there and in other parts of the world. Each side now saw the other as an enemy.

In a speech made in March 1946, the British Prime Minister, Winston Churchill, talked about an "Iron Curtain" in Europe. The Iron Curtain was an imaginary barrier between the West and the **Communist** nations. The phrase meant that Western and Communist countries were deeply divided by different beliefs. The Cold War had begun and spying would play an important role in the battle between East and West.

The Soviet Union

The Soviet Union contained fifteen states called republics. At the end of the Cold War in 1991, the Soviet republics became fifteen independent nations:
- Armenia
- Azerbaijan
- Belarus
- Estonia
- Georgia
- Kazakhstan
- Kyrgyzstan
- Latvia
- Lithuania
- Moldova
- Russia
- Tajikistan
- Turkmenistan
- Ukraine
- Uzbekistan

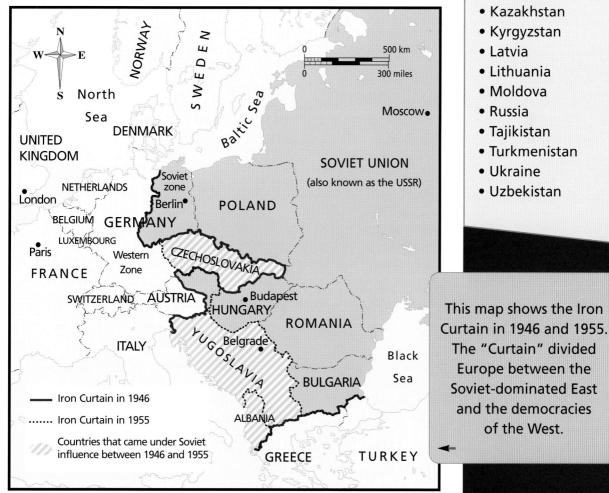

This map shows the Iron Curtain in 1946 and 1955. The "Curtain" divided Europe between the Soviet-dominated East and the democracies of the West.

___ Iron Curtain in 1946

······· Iron Curtain in 1955

▨ Countries that came under Soviet influence between 1946 and 1955

espionage work done by spies to collect information about other countries

Klaus Fuchs and the Manhattan Project

During World War II, scientists from many Western countries developed the atomic bomb (also called **nuclear bomb**). They were working for the American and British governments in Chicago, New Mexico and other laboratories around the United States. Their research was called the "Manhattan Project". The project led to the dropping of atomic bombs on the Japanese cities of Hiroshima and Nagasaki.

Klaus Fuchs was one of the scientists who worked on the Manhattan Project. After leaving Germany before the start of World War II and working in the United Kingdom, he went to the United States in 1943 to work on the atomic bomb. Fuchs was a **Communist**. In 1941, he began spying for the **Soviet Union**. He gave the **Soviets** some of the information they would need to build a nuclear bomb of their own.

Atomic weapons and the Cold War

During the Cold War, several nations built atomic weapons. However, the Americans and the Soviets controlled most of these weapons. Some people feared that the two enemies would start a nuclear war that would have killed millions of people.

The United States dropped an atomic bomb on the Japanese city of Hiroshima on 6 August 1945. These soldiers are standing in the rubble of the destroyed city.

Word Bank nuclear bomb type of weapon that has enormous destructive power

Fuchs tells all

In 1946, Fuchs returned to the United Kingdom from the United States. He continued to spy for the Soviet Union. Three years later, the Soviets tested their first nuclear bomb. Some people in the **West** feared that the Soviets might use nuclear weapons against them. People also suspected that spies had helped the Soviets build their first nuclear bomb.

The **FBI** had proof that Fuchs was one of the spies who had helped the Soviets. In December 1949, an **MI5** agent told Fuchs he was suspected of **espionage**. Spying for a foreign country is a crime. A few weeks later, Fuchs confessed. He spent nine years in a British prison before being freed and returning to East Germany.

Klaus Fuchs was held in a British prison from 1950 to 1959.

The VENONA project

During World War II, the United States had a secret programme called VENONA. It helped the Americans read Soviet intelligence messages. These messages showed that Fuchs (above) and several other workers on the Manhattan Project had spied for the Soviet Union.

Soviet someone from the Soviet Union

Spies across America?

Joseph McCarthy was a US **senator** in the 1950s. McCarthy claimed that **Communists** were working in the US government and in American companies. He said these people might be spies for the **Soviet Union**. The arrest of Klaus Fuchs had shown that the **Soviets** had spied on the Manhattan Project. Many Americans believed McCarthy when he said there were still Communist spies in the United States.

Naming spies

McCarthy named several people who he thought were Communists. Some of the people he mentioned did have contacts with known Communists. But others had no ties with **Communism** or Soviet spies at all. Furthermore, McCarthy never proved that anyone he named actually had given the Soviets **classified** information.

Real spies at work

During the early 1950s, the American government caught many spies. One of them was Julius Rosenberg. Rosenberg, like Klaus Fuchs, had worked on the Manhattan Project. His wife Ethel helped with his spy work and was also arrested. In 1953, the Rosenbergs were executed for spying.

Some Americans who hated Communism called Joseph McCarthy (seen here pointing to a map) a hero.

COMMUNIST PARTY ORGANIZATION U.S.A.-FEB. 9,1950

Word Bank   classified   information that only certain important people are allowed to see

Hunting for Communists

In 1953, McCarthy led a committee to hunt for Communists. His team searched for people who seemed to support Communism. McCarthy also claimed that some soldiers in the US army were spies for the Soviet Union.

Once again, McCarthy could not prove his claims. Some Americans began to doubt what he said. Political leaders who had once supported him began to ignore him. By the end of 1954, McCarthy had lost his influence. However, by this time his unproven accusations had ruined the careers of many prominent Americans. Historians and others still use his name today. The effort during the 1950s to find Americans thought to be Communists is today called "McCarthyism".

> During the late 1940s and early 1950s, many Americans believed that some famous American film stars were Communists including, from left to right, Paul Henreid, Lauren Bacall, Danny Kaye, and Humphrey Bogart. ↓

Cambridge spies

A spy case in the United Kingdom made the news at the same time as Joseph McCarthy was hunting for Communists in the United States. Guy Burgess and Donald Maclean studied at Cambridge University in England. After they left Cambridge, they worked for the British government as spies. In 1951, Burgess and Maclean **defected** to the Soviet Union to avoid arrest for **treason** as they were also spying for the Soviet Union.

---

defect flee one's own country to live in another country with a different form of government

FIRST CONFLICTS

Germany was divided after World War II. The British, Americans, French, and **Soviets** each controlled one area of Germany. They also divided up the German capital of Berlin, which was deep inside the Soviet area.

The Berlin Airlift

The Western nations wanted a **democratic** Germany. The Soviets wanted a **Communist** government in the area under their control. In June 1948, Soviet spies discovered that the Western **Allies** planned to join their areas together, including Berlin. Joseph Stalin, the Soviet leader, was against this. So he decided to **blockade** the roads, railways, and canals that went into West Berlin.

Airlift facts

During the Soviet blockade of parts of Berlin, thousands of tonnes of supplies had to be flown in. Here are some key facts about the Berlin Airlift:

- The population of West Berlin in 1948 was 2.3 million.
- The weight of supplies flown in daily during December 1948 was 4500 tonnes.
- The planes arrived every 90 seconds.
- The most flights in one day was 1398.

The Berlin Airlift continued all through the winter of 1948–1949. Here, workers are unloading the one millionth sack of coal arriving in Berlin.

Word Bank airlift use of many planes to bring people or goods in and out of a place

To defeat the blockade, American and British planes constantly flew in supplies. This **airlift** kept people who lived in West Berlin alive until Stalin ended the blockade in May 1949.

The Korean War

The country of Korea in Asia was also divided after World War II. The **Soviet Union** controlled the North and helped Korean Communists take power there. The Americans controlled South Korea. In June 1950, troops from North Korea invaded the south. The United States did not want Communists to rule South Korea. The **United Nations** asked the United States and other countries to send troops to defend South Korea. China, which had become a Communist nation in 1949, also entered the war, to fight for North Korea. The Korean War ended in 1953 when the Communists failed to defeat South Korea.

Closed society

During the Korean War, the Soviet Union relied on spies such as Donald Maclean and Guy Burgess to find out secret information. The United Kingdom and the United States did not have similar spies working in the Soviet Union. The Soviets tightly controlled their citizens' actions. **CIA** or **MI6 agents** did not have many chances to find Soviets willing to spy for the **West**.

This map shows the countries where Cold War struggles erupted into violence and war.

SOVIET UNION

UNITED KINGDOM — Cambridge
London
Berlin
Moscow
GERMANY
CZECHOSLOVAKIA
HUNGARY
Budapest
AFGHANISTAN
IRAN
PAKISTAN
NORTH KOREA
CHINA
SOUTH KOREA
UNITED STATES OF AMERICA
New York
Washington DC
CUBA
GUATEMALA
EL SALVADOR
NICARAGUA
AFRICA
ETHIOPIA
CONGO
ANGOLA
VIETNAM

0   5000 km (at Equator)
0   3000 miles (at Equator)

Flashpoints during the Cold War

blockade   close all air, sea, and land routes into a city or country

Double agent

George Blake was a British **diplomat** in South Korea. He also spied for **MI6**. When North Korea invaded South Korea in 1950, Blake was taken prisoner. He was released in April 1953. While in prison, Blake decided he liked **Communism** and so he became a **double agent** for the **Soviet Union**.

A secret tunnel

In October 1953, Blake learned about plans to build a tunnel under East Berlin. The British MI6 and American **CIA intelligence** agencies would use the tunnel to **tap Soviet** telephone lines and learn their secrets. Blake told the Soviets about the tunnel, but they did not stop it being built, partly to protect Blake's position.

East German soldiers inside the Berlin spy tunnel after the Soviets and East Germans uncovered it in 1956.

Secret messages

Using the spy tunnel, the British and Americans recorded 443,000 messages on 50,000 reels of recording tape. The Allies learned the location of about 100 Soviet air force bases in the Soviet Union. The messages also named several hundred Soviet spies in East Germany and Moscow.

Word Bank double agent intelligence agent for one country who also spies for another country

The Soviets wanted to make sure that the CIA and MI6 did not guess that they knew about the tunnel. They continued to permit the tapping of phones and allowed the **Allies** to hear a mixture of real and false information.

In April 1956, the Soviets finally uncovered and closed the spy tunnel that had been completed in 1955. They acted as if they had not known about it before. With the closing of the tunnel, the **West** lost an important method of tapping into Soviet secret messages.

Spy uncovered

Blake continued to act as a double agent. In 1961, the British finally found out that he was helping the Soviets and arrested him. He went to prison in England, but later escaped. He eventually ended up living in Moscow, in the Soviet Union.

The Berlin Wall

Many East Germans wanted to escape Communism. They came to East Berlin and then crossed into the western half of the city. In 1961, the East Germans built a wall between East and West Berlin. East Germans who tried to cross the wall were shot. The Berlin Wall reminded people around the world that Communist governments limited freedom.

This photo shows the Berlin Wall in 1962. It was designed to keep East and West Berlin separate. It was knocked down in 1989.

tap hidden device used to hear other people's telephone calls

Trouble in Hungary

The **Soviet Union** tried to keep tight control over other **Warsaw Pact** nations (see panel on left). The **KGB** and **GRU** had **agents** in those countries. Their job was to make sure **Communists** always controlled the governments.

Hungary was a member of the Warsaw Pact. In October 1956, some Hungarians began to protest against their government. They wanted other political parties besides the Communist Party. They also wanted the freedom to say and write what they liked. The Hungarians were tired of hearing only Communist **propaganda**. The protesters fought with police. **Soviet** troops marched into Hungary to end the protests, but the protesters kept on fighting.

In this photo, armed Hungarians stand in front of a military vehicle showing the national flag during the 1956 rebellion.

NATO North Atlantic Treaty Organization, a group of Western nations led by the United States

The KGB takes charge

The Soviets made a man called Imre Nagy the new leader of Hungary. However, Nagy soon began to support some of the protesters. He wanted to weaken Soviet control in Hungary. The Soviets sent KGB leader Ivan Serov to the Hungarian capital of Budapest. The Soviets said Serov had come to give the new Hungarian government advice. Instead, he and his agents planned to end Nagy's rule.

On 3 November 1956, Serov and his men burst into a room filled with Hungary's leaders. The KGB arrested the Hungarians. A new leader called Matyas Rakosi, who followed Soviet orders, took over the government. Nagy was arrested and killed. Thousands of other Hungarians were killed or wounded during the **rebellion**.

The CIA in action

Like the Soviet **KGB**, the **CIA** in the United States played an important role in shaping foreign governments. In 1953, for example, CIA agents helped to replace Muhammad Musaddiq, the ruler of Iran. The Americans thought he was too friendly with the Soviet Union. In 1954, the CIA helped to force the Guatemalan president, Jacobo Arbenz, out of power. Arbenz was a supporter of the Russians, and had bought weapons from them.

In 1956, these Hungarian protesters drove through the streets of Budapest on top of a tank. Their success was short-lived as the Soviets crushed their rebellion.

propaganda information meant to change how people think or act
Warsaw Pact group of Communist nations controlled by the Soviet Union

TOOLS OF THE TRADE

On 1 May 1960, Francis Gary Powers soared 20,730 metres (68,000 feet) above the **Soviet Union** in a U-2 plane. Powers was a spy who worked for the **CIA**. Inside his plane was a special camera that he used to photograph **Soviet military** sites.

Shot down and caught

Suddenly, a Soviet missile exploded near the plane and it began to fall. The Americans did not know that the Soviets had any missiles that could reach this height. As Powers' plane burned, he used a **parachute** to escape the flames. Powers carried a needle with poison on its tip. He was supposed to kill himself so he would not be caught, but Powers did not use the needle and he was arrested by the Soviet **KGB**.

The Americans at first denied that Powers was a spy. The Soviets then showed them maps that Powers had carried which proved that he was a spy. The Soviets were very angry that the Americans had sent spy planes over the Soviet Union and they sent Powers to prison.

U-2 facts

Here is a look at America's "spy in the sky", the U-2 spy plane:

Length:
19.2 metres (63 feet)

Height:
4.8 metres (16 feet)

Wingspan:
32 metres (105 feet)

Speed:
more than 764 km/h (475 mph)

Range:
beyond 11,270 km/h (7000 miles)

Altitude:
above 21,212 metres (70,000 feet)

Crew: 1

US pilots flew the U-2 spy plane throughout the Cold War to take secret photographs high above other countries.

Word Bank   parachute   device that slows down a falling object so it can land safely

US pilot Francis Gary Powers (standing), faces a Soviet court after his capture for spying from a U-2 plane.

Spy swap

Around the time that Powers was in prison, the Americans were holding a Soviet spy called Rudolf Abel. The Americans offered to let him go, if the Soviets released Powers. In 1962, the Soviets agreed. Powers returned to the United States. For a while, he worked as a test pilot, flying new planes. However, he later died in a helicopter crash in 1977. Rudolf Abel returned home to the Soviet Union.

Be prepared

In May 1960, US President Dwight Eisenhower explained why the U-2 flights took place:

"We must have knowledge of military forces and preparations around the world, especially those capable of massive surprise attack."

Sputnik enters space

During the 1950s, both the United States and the **Soviet Union** built many large missiles. In May 1957, the **Soviets** tested their first **intercontinental ballistic missile (ICBM)**. In October 1957, the Soviets fired one of these new missiles into space. It carried a **satellite** called *Sputnik*. The launch of *Sputnik* shocked the US government. American leaders realized that the Soviets now had a powerful missile that could attack the United States with nuclear **warheads**.

The "space race"

The Americans soon built their own ICBMs. The United States also launched its own satellites and made plans to explore space. Americans wanted to win the "space race". They wanted to land a person on the moon before the Soviets did.

This photo shows the US *Atlas* rocket on its launchpad. The rocket was used to launch ICBMs. ➡

Word Bank intercontinental ballistic missile (ICBM) missile that can travel more than 5600 kilometres (3500 miles) and carry one or more nuclear weapons

Spying in space

Satellites played an important role in Cold War spying. In August 1960, the Americans launched *Corona*. It took pictures of the Soviet Union and other **Communist** countries. The film from its camera returned to Earth on a **parachute**. *Corona* circled more than 160 kilometres (100 miles) above the Earth. It was so high up that Soviet missiles could not shoot it down.

The Soviet Union soon built its own spy satellites. Later spy satellites broadcast pictures directly back to Earth. Satellites helped both sides learn more about each other. They also meant that the countries did not have to risk losing as many spy planes or **agents**.

Sputnik and *Corona*

This chart compares the *Sputnik* and *Corona* satellites:

Sputnik (Soviet Union)

Launched: 4 October 1957

Name: means "fellow traveller"

Altitude: 800 kilometres (500 miles)

Speed: 28,800 km/h (18,000 mph)

Corona (United States)

Launched: 18 August 1960

Name: means "crown"

Altitude: more than 160 kilometres (100 miles)

Speed: more than 27,000 km/h (17,000 mph)

The US satellite *Corona* took this picture of the Kremlin in the heart of Moscow, the Soviet capital.

warhead part of a missile that explodes

Bugged!

Despite the development of new technology like spy planes and **satellites**, human **agents** remained very important. In 1976, US **CIA** agent Antonio Mendez went to Moscow in the **Soviet Union**. He was an artist who created disguises. He helped the CIA work with a **Soviet double agent** called TRINITY.

Americans who were secret CIA agents in Moscow were almost always under **surveillance**. Soviet **KGB** agents followed them all the time. Tiny devices called **bugs** heard most of what the Americans said at home and work. US agents looked for ways to avoid the KGB, and Mendez helped with this.

Hidden tools

Cold War spies disguised their tools as common items anyone might carry. Here are some real-life examples:

- a gun was disguised to look like a cigarette case
- a coin hid a tiny knife inside
- an umbrella was actually a camera
- a filling in a tooth could hold a tiny message called a microdot.

Spies sometimes used tiny guns to defend themselves. This gun is so small it will fit into a cigarette packet.

Word Bank   **bugs** tiny listening devices that secretly record what people say
putty soft material used to disguise a person's face

Clever disguise

Mendez created a disguise for an American agent meeting TRINITY. Mendez gave the CIA man a brown wig to wear. He put **putty** on the secret agent's nose to make it wider. Then he put a fake moustache on the man's face. Finally, he gave the agent clothes that a Soviet worker would wear. The agent wore these under his Western clothes, which he later removed so he would look like a Russian. The disguise worked. The agent safely met TRINITY. Mendez and other CIA artists then used similar disguises with other agents.

The death of TRINITY

Somehow the KGB learned that TRINITY was a spy. They arrested him in 1977. TRINITY killed himself after he was caught. The spy bit into a pen he carried, which was filled with poison. He did not want to be tortured and forced to reveal what he had told the CIA.

A rare rock

Agents who worked with TRINITY used a special spy tool. They placed instructions and camera film in a hollow rock. TRINITY found the rock and whatever his contacts had left inside. When spies trade items this way without seeing each other, it is called a "dead drop".

Moscow's Kremlin was the home of the Soviet government and many spies held meetings there.

surveillance   close watch by an agent of a person or thing

CRISIS IN CUBA

The CIA in Cuba

The CIA tried to kill Fidel Castro many times. For example, it sent poisoned cigars to the Cuban leader. The CIA also worked with rebels in Cuba. They called this effort "Operation Mongoose". The rebels blew up trains and buildings that were important to the Cuban economy. However, these actions did not force Castro out of power.

Cuba is just 145 kilometres (90 miles) away from the United States. In 1959, Fidel Castro became leader of the country and he ended American influence over Cuba. He took land that was held by US companies and traded with the **Soviet Union**. The Americans were worried that Cuba would become a **Soviet** ally. To prevent this, the **CIA** trained Cuban rebels to fight Castro. In 1961, the rebels invaded a place called the Bay of Pigs but Castro's army defeated the rebels.

Finding soviet missiles

In October 1962, a U-2 spy plane took pictures of Cuba. They showed Soviet nuclear missiles on the island. American President John F. Kennedy told the Soviets to remove the missiles. He did not want nuclear weapons so close to the United States. Soviet leader, Nikita Khrushchev, refused.

Fidel Castro (centre, with beard) and a group of rebels took power from Cuban leaders who had been friendly with the United States.

Preventing a war

People around the world were frightened that the United States and the Soviet Union would go to war because of the missiles in Cuba. Both Kennedy and Khrushchev knew how terrible a nuclear war between their countries would be.

The two leaders held secret talks as their troops prepared to fight. The Soviet Union finally agreed to remove its missiles from Cuba. In return for this, the United States promised not to invade Cuba. The Americans also removed nuclear weapons from Turkey that were aimed at the Soviet Union. The crisis in Cuba could have led to a disastrous war, but it ended peacefully.

Strong words

On 22 October 1962, President Kennedy explained to the world the American response to the Soviet missiles in Cuba.

"Any hostile move anywhere in the world against the safety and freedom of peoples to whom we are committed ... will be met by whatever action is needed ... the greatest danger of all would be to do nothing."

MISSILE TRANSPORTERS

12 PROB GLADELINE MISSILES

HEAVY EQUIPMENT

5 MISSILE DOLLIES

20 LONG CYLINDRICAL TANKS

MISSILE TRANSPORTERS

This photo from a U-2 spy plane, taken in October 1962, shows the Soviet missiles in Cuba.

OPEN STORAGE

A daring request

The date was 12 August 1960. A man named Oleg Penkovsky stopped two American tourists in the streets of Moscow, capital of the **Soviet Union**. Penkovsky was a colonel in the **GRU**, a **Soviet intelligence** agency. He gave the Americans a letter to give to US officials in Moscow. Penkovsky wanted to become a **double agent**.

Nuclear facts

Penkovsky soon met with **agents** from the American **CIA** and British **MI6**. He told them about Soviet nuclear weapons. Penkovsky said that the Soviets did not have many **accurate** missiles. He also gave them details about the SS-4 missiles, which were later sent to Cuba. Penkovsky had information the **West** could not learn in other ways.

The Soviet Union wanted the West to think that missiles such as these were accurate. Oleg Penkovsky told the West that this was not always true.

Word Bank

accurate able to hit a target
code patterns of letters or numbers used to send secret messages

End of a spy

In 1962, Soviet officials began to suspect that Penkovsky was a spy. They hid a tiny camera in his apartment. It showed that Penkovsky had a spy camera and several books of code. Soviet agents then gave Penkovsky a poison that made him ill. While he stayed in hospital, the agents searched his apartment where they found his cameras and code books.

The **KGB** finally arrested Penkovsky during the Cuban Missile Crisis. He was charged with **treason** and was executed in 1963. Penkovsky always knew he risked death if he was caught spying. But he once said he wanted to be a "soldier-warrior for the cause of Truth".

After the death of Penkovsky (far left), rumours spread that Soviet officials had burned him alive as a punishment for his treason. In reality, he was shot.

strategy plans for doing something

THE SUPER SPIES

During the Cold War, the **Soviet Union** and United States used other countries as **proxies**. Proxy nations fought for the **superpowers** or helped them in other ways. The proxy nations produced several "super spies". These spies collected useful information over many years.

Gunter Guillaume

Gunter Guillaume was a super spy. The East German **intelligence** service, the *Stasi*, sent him to West Germany in 1956. He later helped the West German leader Willy Brandt and carried out political **espionage**. He gave the **Soviets** information about Brandt's political goals. Guillaume was caught in 1974. He was later swapped for two West German spies held in East Germany.

Cold War helpers

Some countries not in **NATO** or the **Warsaw Pact** still took part in the Cold War. These included:

Helping the United States
- South Africa
- South Korea
- South Vietnam
- Philippines
- Australia
- Israel
- Taiwan
- Honduras
- El Salvador
- New Zealand
- Thailand
- Japan

Helping the Soviet Union
- Cuba
- North Korea
- North Vietnam
- Nicaragua
- Ethiopia
- Syria
- China

Gunter Guillaume (right) worked closely with West German leader Willy Brandt (left). However, Guillaume was also a super spy working for East Germany.

Word Bank   intercept steal or see a message before it reaches its receiver
mole double agent working inside an intelligence agency or a government

Markus Wolf

Guillaume's boss in East Germany was Markus Wolf. He placed several thousand East German spies in the West. He was sometimes called "the man without a face" as he avoided having his picture taken. He did not want Western **agents** to know what he looked like. Once the Cold War ended, his appearance became known.

The Polish mole

Another super spy was Ryszard Kuklinski. He was a Polish colonel. For almost ten years, Kuklinski was a **mole** for the **West**. In 1981, Kuklinski left Poland and moved to the United States. American officials protected him so **Communist** agents would not try to kill him.

Satellite dishes helped countries intercept messages from both the **Allies** and their enemies.

Spying on friends

Even countries that are allies do not always tell each other everything they do. Friendly nations still sometimes spy on each other. As early as 1945, for example, the United States **intercepted** messages sent by **diplomats** from friendly countries. During the 1980s, on the other hand, Israel received US secrets from an American called Jonathan Pollard.

proxies people or countries working for another person or country
superpower nation with a large army and many nuclear weapons

Double agent

The **Soviet Union** sent Dmitri Polyakov to New York in 1951. He began spying on the United States while working at the **United Nations** (**UN**). Polyakov did his job very well. But he began to dislike the **Soviet** government. He thought the Soviet leaders did not care enough about their citizens.

So, in 1961, Polyakov became a **double agent** for the United States. He met with an American **FBI agent** while on a sea voyage and told him the names of many Soviet **intelligence** agents all around the world. Polyakov soon became a top double agent for the **West**.

The United Nations

The United Nations (UN) was created in 1945. Countries sent **diplomats** to the United Nations to discuss world problems. The nations hoped that this would help to prevent wars. However, some countries sent intelligence agents to work at the United Nations. They could spy while pretending to be diplomats.

The United Nations meets at this building in New York. During the Cold War, Soviet and US officials there often argued with each other.

Word Bank   biological weapons   weapons that cause illness or death by spreading terrible germs or diseases

Useful information

During the Cold War, both the United States and the Soviet Union created dangerous **chemical** and **biological weapons**. Polyakov played an important role in the intelligence about these weapons. The United States used Polyakov to give the Soviets false information about US chemical and biological weapons. The Americans hoped the Soviets would then waste time and money creating chemical weapons that would not work. Polyakov also told the Americans about the weapons created by Soviet scientists.

The game is up

In 1985, a double agent working for the Soviet Union told the Russians that Polyakov was spying for the Americans. By this time, Polyakov had returned to the Soviet Union where he was executed for **treason**.

Code names

Intelligence agencies often give their spies code names.

Spies for the Soviet Union:

Klaus Fuchs – codename: Charles
Guy Burgess – codenames: Madchen, Paul
Julius Rosenberg – codename: Liberal

Spies for the West:

Oleg Penkovsky – codenames: Hero, Yoga
Dmitri Polyakov – codenames: Top Hat, Bourbon

During the Cold War, American soldiers were trained to cope with dangerous chemical and biological weapons. American spies tried to keep the **military** well informed about new weapons, so that US forces could be prepared.

chemical weapons   harmful gases or liquids that are used during war

DIFFICULT DECADES

The Ho Chi Minh Trail

The North Vietnamese built a trail to South Vietnam through the neighbouring countries of Laos and Cambodia. They named it after their leader, Ho Chi Minh. The CIA placed **sensors** along the trail to try to detect movement of enemy troops and equipment. However, the information from the sensors did not help the Americans shut down the Ho Chi Minh Trail.

For many years, the Asian country of Vietnam was ruled by France. However, in 1954, the people of Vietnam won their freedom and the country was split in two. Communists controlled the northern part of the country and were supported by the **Soviet Union** and China. The leaders of South Vietnam, however, hated **Communism** and received help from the United States. The United States hoped this help would keep Communists out of South Vietnam and neighbouring countries.

The Vietnam War

In the late 1950s, Communist **guerrillas** in South Vietnam began fighting their government. The guerrillas were called the "Viet Cong". North Vietnam sent them weapons and supplies.

South Vietnamese troops attack a Viet Cong village in South Vietnam. →

Word Bank   combat troops soldiers trained to actively fight a war
guerrillas   soldiers who do not belong to a regular army

Later, soldiers from North Vietnam helped the Viet Cong fight government forces in South Vietnam.

To help South Vietnam, the United States sent lots of weapons and people to train the South Vietnamese in fighting techniques. However, this was not enough to defeat the Communists. So, in 1965, the United States sent **combat troops** to Vietnam. US soldiers fought there for almost ten years. Fighting also spread from Vietnam to the neighbouring countries of Laos and Cambodia.

Spying in Vietnam

US **intelligence** agencies worked closely with the South Vietnamese. Together they tried to locate Viet Cong leaders. The **CIA** also recruited Laotian soldiers to fight. These soldiers fought troops from North Vietnam that entered Laos.

US troops in Vietnam

The number of US troops in Vietnam grew quickly after 1963.

1959	760
1963	16,000
1966	385,300
1968	536,000
1971	156,800
1973	50
1975	Last troops leave Saigon, the capital of South Vietnam

sensors small devices that detect sound, light, or motion

Helping the enemy

Intelligence played an important role in the Vietnam War for both sides. One very important spy for the **Communists** was a US sailor called John Walker. He worked in the radio room at an important naval office. In 1967, he met some **Soviet diplomats** and offered to give them secret **codes**. He wanted money in return. With the codes, the Soviets learned the location of many American ships. Walker's information also helped the Soviets in Vietnam. American planes often bombed targets in North Vietnam. Thanks to Walker, the Communists knew which targets would be hit and could move soldiers and supplies out of the area.

> The Soviet Union was able to track US ships and submarines using the codes supplied by Walker and his fellow spies.

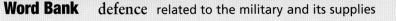

Word Bank defence related to the military and its supplies

Finding more spies

Walker was an excellent spy. The American navy did not realize what he was doing to harm the United States. After several years, Walker asked his brother and a friend in the navy to spy for the Soviets as well. Walker's brother worked for a **defence** company. The two new spies were also paid for their work. Later, Walker's son, also a sailor, joined this **spy ring**.

Millions of secrets

American leaders did not learn about the spy ring until 1985. By then, the Walker spies had helped the Soviets read more than one million US messages. The **KGB** later said that Walker was its most important spy during the Cold War.

A source of spies

The Soviet Union employed several spies in the US **military**. These spies did not believe in Communism, as many other Soviet spies in the **West** did. They just wanted to make money and thought spying was an easy way to do this. At one time, John Walker earned $4000 a month for his **espionage**.

John Walker (front left) was sent to prison for life in 1985 for helping the Soviets. The other three members of his spy ring were also imprisoned for **treason**.

spy ring group of spies who work together

Trouble in Afghanistan

In 1979, the **Soviet Union** supported the government in neighbouring Afghanistan. However, the country's leader, Hafizullah Amin, wanted to improve relations with the **West**. This angered the **Soviets** so the **KGB** sent in special **agents** to kill him.

Communists opposed all religions and most people in Afghanistan practised a religion called **Islam**. They did not want to be ruled by Soviet Communists so the Afghan **Muslims** fought against the Soviet-backed Afghan government, and Soviet troops had to be left in Afghanistan to keep the peace.

Before 1979, the United States and the Soviet Union had been trying to improve their relations with each other. But the Soviet invasion of Afghanistan angered US President Jimmy Carter. He began to help the Afghans. Ronald Reagan also helped Afghanistan after he became president in 1981.

Sports and the Cold War

The 1980 Summer Olympics were held in Moscow. The United States did not send its athletes to the Olympic Games. It was protesting against the Soviet invasion of Afghanistan. Four years later, the Games were held in Los Angeles in the United States. This time the Soviet Union and its allies did not go.

The Soviet Union sent its troops into Afghanistan to keep the peace after Russian KGB agents killed Hafizullah Amin, the leader of Afghanistan.

Word Bank   Islam religion based on the ideas of an Arab named Muhammad, set down in a book called the Qu'ran more than 1500 years ago

Soviet control

The United States helped the people of Afghanistan in many ways and sent weapons and equipment to the Muslim fighters. The rebels fought both the Soviets and the Afghan army, which was being controlled by the Soviets. The Soviets were in charge of the cities, so the rebels lived in the mountains.

Russia leaves

The fighting lasted for many years. The Afghan fighters would launch quick attacks on the Soviets and then return to the mountains. However, in 1989, the Soviet Union decided it had spent too much money and lost too many soldiers fighting in Afghanistan and removed its troops.

Between 1979 and 1989, Afghan Muslims of all ages fought against the Soviets. ↓

The Taliban

During the 1990s, Afghan Muslims called the Taliban took power in Afghanistan. They supported a **terrorist** named Osama bin Laden. Pakistanis who worked with the **CIA** had trained him to fight the Soviets. On September 11 2001, bin Laden's terrorist group attacked the United States. Almost 3000 Americans were killed when the World Trade Center was brought crashing down.

Muslims   followers of Islam
terrorist   person who uses violence for political or religious goals

REACHING THE END

Nuclear weapons

Here is one estimate of the number of nuclear weapons the Soviets and Americans had in 1983:

United States

ICBMs	2242
Submarine-based missiles	5208
Bomber-based warheads	5663
Total	**13,113**

Soviet Union

ICBMs	6993
Submarine-based missiles	1947
Bomber-based warheads	764
Total	**9704**

In 1982, US President Ronald Reagan referred to the **Soviet Union** as an "evil empire". He often talked about ending **Communism** around the world. The **KGB** decided that Reagan was planning a nuclear war against the Soviet Union. It used the code name RYAN for this possible attack.

Oleg Gordievsky

Oleg Gordievsky worked for the KGB in London. He was also a **mole** for Britain's **MI6**. He and other **Soviet agents** were told to watch for signs that the **West** was preparing for war. The KGB thought government workers might stay late at their offices if they were planning an attack, or hospitals might start collecting more blood than usual. The blood would be used to treat the wounded.

US nuclear missiles such as this *Lance* missile could have been used in Eastern Europe in a war against the Soviet Union and its **Communist** allies.
➤

Word Bank narrow-minded only able to see things from one point of view

Ending the fears

Soviet fears about RYAN increased in November 1983. NATO troops held **war games** in Europe. Soviet leaders thought the games were a trick and the West actually planned to attack.

Gordievsky knew that Soviet leaders really believed RYAN could happen. He worried that they might start a nuclear war to prevent a NATO attack. Gordievsky knew that the Soviets and the West could destroy most of the world if there were a war so he told Western officials about RYAN. The Americans saw that their tough talk and actions had worried the Soviets. President Reagan decided to try to improve relations with the Soviet Union.

A crazy idea

Oleg Gordievsky described the British reaction to RYAN:

"They simply couldn't believe that the Soviet leadership was so stupid and **narrow-minded** as to believe in something so impossible."

Towards the end of the Cold War, the United States and the Soviet Union destroyed their **intercontinental ballistic missiles**. In 1987, these American soldiers are using explosives to destroy nose cones from two missiles.

war games training that prepares soldiers for a real war

Getting rid of weapons

During the 1980s, the United States produced many new weapons. **Soviet** leader Mikhail Gorbachev knew his country did not have the money to build as many weapons as the United States. The Soviet leader therefore met with US President Ronald Reagan to discuss **arms control**. They both agreed to get rid of some of their nuclear weapons.

The Wall comes down

Gorbachev also began to change the **Soviet Union's** role in Eastern Europe. He gave the **Warsaw Pact** countries more **independence**. By 1989, most of them had rejected **Communism**. The Berlin Wall (see page 15) was knocked down that year and, in 1990, East and West Germany

Ronald Reagan (centre) and Mikhail Gorbachev (left) met several times. Here they are in Moscow in 1988.

Word Bank   arms control   efforts to limit the number of weapons a country owns

End of the Soviet Union

The desire for greater freedom also spread to the Soviet Union. Starting in 1990, some Soviet republics demanded independence. By the end of 1991, the Soviet Union had ceased to exist and the Cold War was over.

Spies and the Cold War

In the 1990s, several countries released information about their spying activities during the Cold War. However, the United States kept looking for Americans who had helped the Soviets. In 2001, FBI agent Robert Hanssen was arrested for spying during the Cold War. Other spies were caught as well and face jail sentences for **treason**.

Spies today

The Cold War is over, but the West and Russia still use spies. Many play a role in the war against **terrorists**. The **CIA** and the US **military** have special planes that fly without pilots. These planes can take photos or fire missiles.

Many people celebrated the fall of the Berlin Wall in 1989. Here, East German soldiers watch as a crowd of people eagerly wait for the wall to come down.

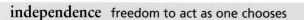

independence freedom to act as one chooses

TIMELINE

1917 **Communists** take control of the Russian government.

1939 World War II begins.

1945 The United States drops the world's first two **nuclear bombs** on Hiroshima and Nagasaki.

World War II ends and the Cold War begins.

The **United Nations** is formed.

1948 US and British planes bring supplies to West Berlin.

1949 The United States and eleven other Western nations form **NATO**.

Communists take power in China.

1950 Klaus Fuchs admits he spied for the **Soviet Union**.

Joseph McCarthy accuses many US government workers of spying for the Soviet Union.

North Korea uses **Soviet** help to invade South Korea.

1951 Guy Burgess and Donald Maclean **defect** from the United Kingdom to Moscow.

1953 Julius and Ethel Rosenberg are executed for **espionage** in the United States.

The **CIA** helps replace the government in Iran.

The Korean War ends.

1954 The CIA defeats a government in Guatemala that works with Communists.

Vietnam is divided into two nations.

1955 The **West** opens a spy tunnel under East Berlin.

The Soviet Union and seven other Communist nations form the **Warsaw Pact**.

1956 Soviet forces and **KGB** agents help end protests against Communist rule in Hungary.

1957	The Soviet Union launches the first **satellite** into space.
1959	Fidel Castro takes over the Cuban government.
1960	Francis Gary Powers is shot down in a U-2 spy plane over the Soviet Union.
	The United States launches the world's first spy satellite.
1961	The CIA helps rebels invade Cuba but the rebels are defeated.
	The Soviets and East Germans build the Berlin Wall.
1962	The Soviet Union places nuclear missiles in Cuba, sparking the Cuban Missile Crisis.
	A U-2 spy plane notices the missiles. The Soviets agree to remove them.
	Soviet **double agent** Oleg Penkovsky is arrested for spying for the West.
1965	American **combat troops** arrive in South Vietnam.
1975	The Vietnam War ends.
1979	KGB **agents** kill the leader of Afghanistan and Soviet troops invade the country.
1985	Mikhail Gorbachev comes to power in the Soviet Union.
1987	The United States and the Soviet Union agree to remove many nuclear weapons from Europe.
1989	Communist governments fall in several Eastern European countries.
	The Berlin Wall is torn down.
1991	The Cold War ends.

FIND OUT MORE

44

Search tips

There are billions of pages on the Internet so it can be difficult to find exactly what you are looking for. These search skills will help you find useful websites more quickly:

- Use simple keywords instead of whole sentences.

- Use two to six keywords in a search, putting the most important words first.

- Be precise – only use names of people, places or things.

- If you want to find words that go together, put quote marks around them.

Books

Here are a few of the many books about spying and the Cold War.

The Causes of the Cold War, by Stewart Ross (Hodder Wayland, 2001)
An analysis of why the Cold War began giving a clear account of East-West relations from the end of World War II to the end of the Korean War.

The Cold War, by David Taylor (Heinemann, 2001)
Explores the issues and introduces the leaders and key figures of this key historical era.

The Cold War, by Sean Sheehan (Hodder Wayland, 2003)
An excellent overview of the global struggle that threatened the stability of the whole planet.

The Cuban Missile Crisis, by Peter Chrisp (Hodder Wayland, 2002)
Gives a history of Cuba before October 1962, and details of the missile crisis.

The End of the Cold War, by Christine Hatt (Hodder Wayland, 2001)
The compelling story of the changing relationship between the United States and the Soviet Union during the 1970s and 1980s, which ended in the collapse of Communism in Eastern Europe.

Tales of Real Spies, by Fergus Fleming (Usborne, 1997)
Explores the adventures of several spies before and during the Cold War.

DVD/VHS

Films about the Cold War are normally aimed at an adult audience, and can be upsetting. Ask a parent or teacher before watching these.

The Birth of the Cold War (VHS, 1997)

Cambridge Spies (DVD, 2003)

Declassified: The Inside Story of American Espionage Agencies (VHS, 2000)

Secrets, Lies and Atomic Spies (VHS, 2002)

Websites

Search tips

Most sites are aimed at adults and may contain upsetting information and pictures. Make sure that you use well-known sites with correct information, such as the ones below.

http://www.pbs.org/wnet/innovation/about_episode3.html
Website related to a TV show about US spy agencies and some famous Cold War spies.

http://www.cnn.com/SPECIALS/cold.war/experience/spies/
Photos and information on spies, their tools, and important missions.

http://www.coldwar.org/
Online museum with links to other Cold War sites.

http://www.crimelibrary.com/terrorists_spies/spies/index.html
Information on the Cambridge Five and other Cold War spies.

http://www.cia.gov/cia/ciakids/index.shtml
A CIA website for students.

http://www.fbi.gov/libref/historic/famcases/famcases.htm
The FBI explains how it caught several foreign spies and double agents.

Where to search

Search engine

A search engine looks through the entire web and lists all sites that match the words in the search box. It can give thousands of links, but the best matches are at the top of the list, on the first page. Try **bbc.co.uk/search**

Search directory

A search directory is like a library of websites that have been sorted by a person instead of a computer. You can search by keyword or subject and browse through the different sites like you look through books on a library shelf. A good example is **yahooligans.com**

GLOSSARY

accurate able to hit a target

agents spies or people who work with spies and help gather intelligence

airlift use of many planes to bring people or goods in and out of a place

Allies Western countries, including the United Kingdom and the United States, that were friends and worked closely together

arms control efforts to limit the number of weapons a country owns

biological weapons weapons that cause illness or death by spreading terrible germs or diseases

blockade close all air, sea, and land routes into a city or country

bugs tiny listening devices that secretly record what people say

capitalism economic system that allows people to own property and business

CIA (Central Intelligence Agency) leading American intelligence agency responsible for national security in the United States

chemical weapons harmful gases or liquids that are used during war

classified information that only certain important people are allowed to see

code patterns of letters or numbers used to send secret messages

combat troops soldiers trained to actively fight a war

Communism political system controlled by one party that limits personal freedom. Communists believe in this system.

counter-intelligence efforts by one country to prevent other countries from spying on it

defect flee one's own country to live in another country with a different form of government

defence related to the military and its supplies

democracy political system that allows people to elect their leaders

diplomat person who helps shape a country's relations with foreign nations

double agent intelligence agent for one country who also spies for another country

espionage work done by spies to collect information about other countries

FBI (Federal Bureau of Investigation) leading American intelligence agency mainly responsible for protecting the United States from terrorist attack

GRU (Main Intelligence Administration) East German intelligence agency

guerrillas soldiers who do not belong to a regular army

independence freedom to act as one chooses

intelligence government services that spy on other countries; also, the information spies gather

intercept steal or see a message before it reaches its receiver

intercontinental ballistic missile (ICBM) missile that can travel more than 5600 kilometres (3500 miles) and carry one or more nuclear weapons

Islam religion based on the ideas of an Arab named Muhammad, set down in a book called the Qu'ran more than 1500 years ago

KGB (Committee for State Security) leading intelligence agency in the Soviet Union

military country's fighting forces, including army, navy, and air force

MI5 (Military Intelligence 5) British agency responsible for protecting the United Kingdom against threats to its national security

MI6 (Military Intelligence 6) secret intelligence service working for the British government. Known as "The Firm".

mole double agent working inside an intelligence agency or a government

Muslims followers of Islam

narrow-minded only able to see things from one point of view

NATO (North Atlantic Treaty Organization) group of Western nations led by the United States

nuclear bomb type of weapon that has enormous destructive power

parachute device that slows down a falling object so it can land safely

propaganda information meant to change how people think or act

proxies people or countries working for another person or country

putty soft material used to disguise a person's face

rebellion use of violence to force a change in government

satellite object that circles the Earth sending back various kinds of information

senator one of 100 people elected to serve in the American Senate

sensors small devices that detect sound, light, or motion

Soviet someone from the Soviet Union

Soviet Union country that once spread across northern Asia into Eastern Europe and included what is now Russia

spy ring group of spies who work together

strategy plans for doing something

superpower nation with a large army and many nuclear weapons

surveillance close watch by an agent of a person or thing

tap hidden device used to hear other people's telephone calls

terrorist person who uses violence for political or religious goals

treason harm or destroy one's own government

tried put on trial for a crime

United Nations (UN) large group of countries that work together to prevent or end wars

war games training that prepares soldiers for a real war

warhead part of a missile that explodes

Warsaw Pact group of Communist nations controlled by the Soviet Union

West countries of Western Europe and North America

INDEX